PUN
CTU
ATE
IT!

QUOTATION MARKS AND APOSTROPHES

BY KATE RIGGS
ILLUSTRATED BY RANDALL ENOS

CREATIVE EDUCATION • CREATIVE PAPERBACKS

Published by Creative Education and Creative Paperbacks
P.O. Box 227, Mankato, Minnesota 56002
Creative Education and Creative Paperbacks are
imprints of The Creative Company
www.thecreativecompany.us

Design and production by Liddy Walseth
Art direction by Rita Marshall
Printed in the United States of America

Illustrations by Randall Enos © 2016

Library of Congress Cataloging-in-Publication Data
Riggs, Kate.
Quotation Marks and Apostrophes / by Kate Riggs; illustrated by Randall Enos.
p. cm. — (Punctuate it!)
Includes bibliographical references and index.
Summary: An illustrated guide to the punctuation marks known as quota-
tion marks and apostrophes, including descriptions and examples of how to
properly use them in quotes and in showing possession and contraction.
ISBN 978-1-60818-736-2 (hardcover)
ISBN 978-1-62832-332-0 (pbk)
ISBN 978-1-56660-771-1 (eBook)
1. Apostrophe—Juvenile works. 2. Quotation marks—Juvenile works.
3. English language—Punctuation—Juvenile works.

PE1450.R54 2016
428.2/3—dc23   2016002555

CCSS: L.1.2; L.2.2; L.3.1, 2, 3, 4, 5; L.4. 1, 2, 3, 4; RI.3.1, 2, 7, 8; RI.4.2, 8

First Edition HC 9 8 7 6 5 4 3 2 1
First Edition PBK 9 8 7 6 5 4 3 2 1

TABLE OF CONTENTS

5

INTRODUCTION

6

SAYS WHO?

11

PUNCTUATION PRACTICE

12

WORKING TOGETHER

16

PUNCTUATION PRACTICE

18

YOU BELONG TO ME

24

PUNCTUATION PRACTICE

26

MEAN WHAT YOU SAY

30

ACTIVITY: WHO'S OR WHOSE?

32

GLOSSARY | READ MORE
WEBSITE | INDEX

INTRODUCTION

NOLAN AND MIKAELA
WERE PLAYING A GAME.
MIKAELA WAS WINNING.
NOLAN WASN'T HAP-
PY. "YOU CAN'T MOVE
THERE!" NOLAN SAID
AS MIKAELA TOOK HER
TURN. "IT ISN'T FAIR!"
"DON'T BLAME ME,"
SAID MIKAELA. "I DIDN'T
MAKE UP THE RULES."

SAYS WHO?

*T*here are rules in a game. There are rules in speaking and writing. How we use punctuation is part of those rules. Quotation marks are used to show that someone said or wrote something.

This is called a direct quote. A statement about what someone said is an indirect quote. That doesn't need quotation marks.

"It's your turn, Julie," I said.
I told Julie it was her turn.

In the first **sentence**, I am talking to Julie, so it's a direct quote. The second sentence simply reports that I said something. So it's an indirect quote.

Quotation marks are used in other ways, too. They are used around the titles of short works such as songs, poems, and articles. But quotation marks are not used with titles of books. You don't need them for video games, either. Those titles would be **italicized** instead.

Zach likes to play *Minecraft*.

What would happen if you were talking about a song to your friend? The title of the song should be in quotation marks. But what you say would also be in quotation marks. In such cases, you would use two sets of quotation marks. The second set would be single marks within the first set.

"Let's use 'Bad Blood' to play musical chairs!"

PUNCTUATION PRACTICE:

Quotation marks show when someone is talking. Where should the quotation marks go in the sentence below?

Why can't we play checkers? asked Maggie.

WORKING TOGETHER

Quotation marks have to get along with other punctuation in a sentence. You may have noticed that periods and commas always go inside the closing quotation mark. Question marks and exclamation points go inside most of the time, too.

"Did you move the chess pieces?" asked Sarah.

When you introduce a quote that comes at the end of a sentence, use a comma before the first quotation mark. The comma lets a reader know that something is coming. This is called setting off the quote.

Andy said, "I wish I could play games all day!"

Sometimes a quotation is split. This means that the person speaking is not named at first. The quote is split into two parts. You will need a comma at the end of the first part. You will also need one before the second part.

"Make sure you clean up," Mom said, "or we can't get ice cream."

PUNCTUATION PRACTICE:

What if you had a quote in the middle of a sentence—but no punctuation? Add the missing punctuation marks to help make sense of the following:

Nick teased I'm taking all the Monopoly money and ran away

A: Nick teased, "I'm taking all the Monopoly money!" and ran away.

YOU
BELONG
TO ME

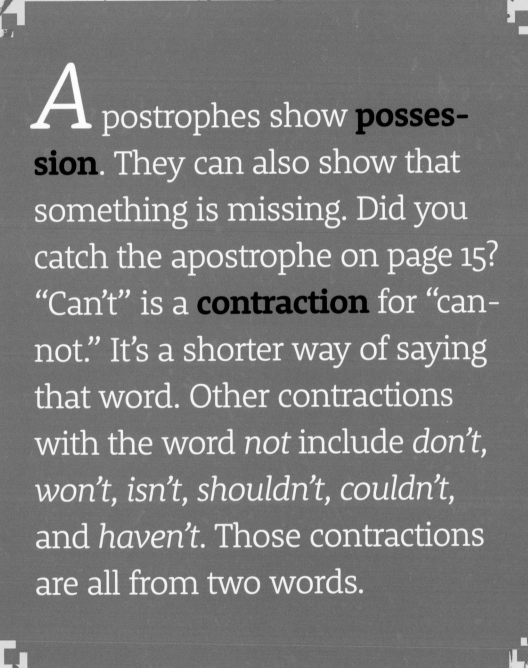

Apostrophes show **possession**. They can also show that something is missing. Did you catch the apostrophe on page 15? "Can't" is a **contraction** for "cannot." It's a shorter way of saying that word. Other contractions with the word *not* include *don't, won't, isn't, shouldn't, couldn't,* and *haven't*. Those contractions are all from two words.

Possessives are shown in two main ways. For a singular noun, you use an apostrophe and an *s*. For most plural nouns, you just add an apostrophe.

Laura's deck of cards flew off the table.

The rabbits' game of tag was interrupted.

What if that second sentence said this instead?

The rabbit's game of tag was interrupted. It wouldn't be a very fun game for one rabbit! Putting the apostrophe in a different place changes the meaning of the whole sentence!

Some plurals do not end in s. They follow the rule for singular possessives.

The children's board games covered the floor.

PUNCTUATION PRACTICE:

Where would you add an apostrophe to show possession in the following sentence?

Did you see Emilys score?

A: Did you see Emily's score?

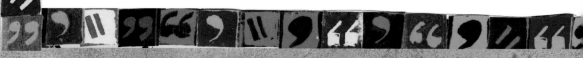

ITS

ITS

ITS

MEAN
WHAT
YOU SAY

W hen it comes to apos-
trophes and quotation
marks, you have to play by
the rules.

Knowing how to use these punctuations is important. Without them, it may be impossible for others to know what you mean!

-ACTIVITY-

WHO'S
OR
WHOSE?

You already know that possessive nouns are made with an apostrophe and an *s*. But pronouns change words entirely! That makes it tricky to figure out possessives and contractions, especially when you h words that sound the same. Use the wo bank at right to fill in the blanks with correct contraction or possessive p Write the answers on your own sheet